POWER NOTES
By Yolanda Walker

No Matter What Color, Age, or Gender you are the Bible is one of the most important Books you will ever read. The Bible has given many knowledge and comfort for their daily living. We pray that you will continue in your spiritual devotion and development. Our prayer is this book will help serve as a tool for reflection of your study of the Word of God. And that it will help bring you closer into your relationship with the Lord through communal and personal study and meditation.

I dedicate this book to my Lord and Savior Jesus Christ and to my parents Winston and Joan Walker for your unconditional love and support. The Morehouse School of Religion of the Interdenominational Theological Center of Atlanta, Georgia for my seminary training. In addition, I dedicate this book to the Faith Community and all churches and pastors who have shepherd and inspired me: Dr. Morgan Babb, Pastors Kenneth and Carlos Jones, Bishop Jerry Maynard, the late Pastor Nathan Simmons, and Pastor Breonus Mitchell. And last but not least my daughter Ashley who keeps me laughing and who has (Justin Bieber) fever.

 This Book Copyright 2013 by Yolanda Walker, Tri-Fold Outreach, P.O. Box 53, Whites Creek, TN 37189, (800)664-1793. Pictures used with permission from Microsoft. ISBN: 9781482045383.

Contents

Sunday School/Bible Study Notes

Sermon Notes

Church Announcements

2013 Calendar

To Do List

Contact List

Hebrews 11:1

"Now Faith is the substance of things hoped for, the evidence of things not seen"

Sunday School Notes: _____ **Date:** _____

_____

_____

_____

_____

_____

_____

_____

_____

_____

_____

_____

_____

_____

Bible Study Notes: _____

_____

_____

_____

_____

_____

_____

_____

_____

_____

_____

2 Corinthians 5:21

"For He made Him who knew no sin to be sin for us, that we might become the righteousness of God in Him."

Speaker_____

Sermon Title: _____ Date:_____

Isaiah 26:3

"You will keep him in perfect peace, Whose mind is stayed on You, Because he trust in You."

Sunday School Notes: _____ Date:_____

_____
_____
_____
_____
_____
_____
_____
_____
_____
_____
_____
_____

Bible Study Notes:

_____
_____
_____
_____
_____
_____
_____
_____
_____
_____
_____

John 8:32, 36

"And you shall know the truth, and the truth shall make you free. Therefore if the Son makes you free, you shall be free indeed."

Speaker_____

Sermon Title: _____Date:_____

Luke 10:19

"Behold, I give you the authority to trample on serpents and scorpions, and over all the power of the enemy, and nothing shall by any means hurt you."

Sunday School Notes: _____ Date:_____

_____
_____
_____
_____
_____
_____
_____
_____
_____
_____
_____
_____

Bible Study Notes:

_____
_____
_____
_____
_____
_____
_____
_____
_____
_____
_____
_____

2 Corinthians 5:17

"Therefore, if anyone is in Christ, he is a new creation; old things have passed away; behold, all things have become new.

Speaker_____

Sermon Title: _____Date:_____

Mark 16:17

"And these signs will follow those who believe: In My name they will cast out demons: they will speak with new tongues."

Sunday School Notes: _____ Date:_____

_____
_____
_____
_____
_____
_____
_____
_____
_____
_____
_____
_____

Bible Study Notes:

_____
_____
_____
_____
_____
_____
_____
_____
_____
_____

Revelation 12:11

"And they overcame him by the blood of the Lamb and by the Word of their testimony, and they did not love their lives to the death."

Speaker_____

Sermon Title: _____Date:_____

Matthew 12:50

"For whoever does the will of My Father in heaven is my brother and sister and mother."

Sunday School Notes: _____ Date:_____

_____
_____
_____
_____
_____
_____
_____
_____
_____
_____
_____
_____

Bible Study Notes:

_____
_____
_____
_____
_____
_____
_____
_____
_____
_____
_____
_____
_____

Philippians 1:21

"For to me, to live is Christ, and to die is gain."

Speaker_____

Sermon Title: _____ Date: _____

Matthew 21:22

"And whatever things you ask in prayer, believing, you will receive."

Sunday School Notes: _____ Date:_____

_____
_____
_____
_____
_____
_____
_____
_____
_____
_____
_____

Bible Study Notes:

_____
_____
_____
_____
_____
_____
_____
_____
_____
_____
_____
_____
_____

2 Timothy 3:16

"All Scripture is given by inspiration of God, and is profitable for doctrine, for reproof, for correction, for instruction in righteousness."

Speaker_____

Sermon Title: _____Date:_____

2 Corinthians 1:20

"For all the promises of God in Him are Yes, and in Him Amen, to the glory of God through us."

Sunday School Notes: _____ Date:_____

_____
_____
_____
_____
_____
_____
_____
_____
_____
_____
_____
_____

Bible Study Notes:

_____
_____
_____
_____
_____
_____
_____
_____
_____
_____
_____
_____

Mark 13:31

"Heaven and earth will pass away, but My words will by no means pass away."

Speaker_____

Sermon Title: _____Date:_____

_____
_____
_____
_____
_____
_____
_____
_____
_____
_____
_____
_____
_____
_____
_____
_____
_____
_____
_____
_____
_____
_____
_____
_____
_____
_____

Psalm 119: 105

"Your word is a lamp to my feet and a light to my path."

Sunday School Notes: _____ Date:_____

_____
_____
_____
_____
_____
_____
_____
_____
_____
_____

Bible Study Notes:

_____
_____
_____
_____
_____
_____
_____
_____
_____
_____
_____

Romans 8:31

"What then shall we say to these things? If God is for us, who can be against us?

Speaker_____

Sermon Title: _____Date:_____

Psalm 46:1

"God is our refuge and strength, A very present help in trouble."

Sunday School Notes: _____ Date:_____

_____
_____
_____
_____
_____
_____
_____
_____
_____
_____
_____

Bible Study Notes:

_____
_____
_____
_____
_____
_____
_____
_____
_____
_____
_____
_____

Romans 3:23

"For all have sinned and fall short of the glory of God."

Speaker_____

Sermon Title: _____Date:_____

John 3:17

"For God did not send His Son into the world to condemn the world, but to save the world through him."

Sunday School Notes: _____ Date: _____

_____
_____
_____
_____
_____
_____
_____
_____
_____
_____
_____

Bible Study Notes:

_____
_____
_____
_____
_____
_____
_____
_____
_____
_____
_____
_____

Proverbs 22:6

"Train up a child in the way he should go, And when he is old he will not depart from it."

Speaker_____

Sermon Title: _____ Date:_____

_____

_____
_____
_____
_____
_____
_____
_____
_____
_____
_____
_____
_____
_____
_____
_____
_____
_____
_____
_____
_____
_____
_____
_____
_____

Psalm 119:105

"Your word is a lamp to my feet, and a light to my path."

Sunday School Notes: _____ Date:_____

_____
_____
_____
_____
_____
_____
_____
_____
_____
_____
_____
_____

Bible Study Notes:

_____
_____
_____
_____
_____
_____
_____
_____
_____
_____
_____
_____
_____
_____

Psalm 37:23

"The steps of a good man are ordered by the Lord, And He delights in his way."

Speaker_____

Sermon Title: _____Date:_____

Matthew 21:22

"And whatever things you ask in prayer, believing, you will receive."

Sunday School Notes: _____ Date: _____

_____
_____
_____
_____
_____
_____
_____
_____
_____
_____
_____

Bible Study Notes:

_____
_____
_____
_____
_____
_____
_____
_____
_____
_____
_____
_____

Jeremiah 33:3

"Call to Me, and I will answer you, and show you great and mighty things, which you do not know."

Speaker_____

Sermon Title: _____ Date:_____

Isaiah 26:3

"You will keep him in perfect peace, Whose mind is stayed on You, Because he trusts in You."

Sunday School Notes: _____ Date: _____

_____
_____
_____
_____
_____
_____
_____
_____
_____
_____

Bible Study Notes:

_____
_____
_____
_____
_____
_____
_____
_____
_____
_____
_____

Revelation 12:11

"And they overcame him by the blood of the Lamb and by the word of their testimony, and they did not love their lives to the death."

Speaker_____

Sermon Title: _____Date:_____

Hebrews 11:1

"Now faith is the substance of things hoped for, the evidence of things not seen."

Sunday School Notes: _____ Date:_____

_____
_____
_____
_____
_____
_____
_____
_____
_____
_____
_____

Bible Study Notes:

_____
_____
_____
_____
_____
_____
_____
_____
_____
_____
_____
_____

Romans 10:17

"So then faith comes by hearing, and hearing by the Word of God."

Speaker_____

Sermon Title: _____ Date:_____

Psalm 34:19

"Many are the afflictions of the righteous, But the Lord delivers him out of them all."

Sunday School Notes: _____ Date:_____

_____
_____
_____
_____
_____
_____
_____
_____
_____
_____
_____

Bible Study Notes:

_____
_____
_____
_____
_____
_____
_____
_____
_____
_____
_____
_____

Romans 8:37

"Yet in all these things we are more than conquerors through Him who loved us."

Speaker_____

Sermon Title: _____Date:_____

_____

Philippians 1:6

"Being confident of this very thing, that He who has begun a good work in you will complete it until the day of Jesus Christ."

Sunday School Notes: _____ Date:_____

_____
_____
_____
_____
_____
_____
_____
_____
_____
_____
_____
_____
_____
_____

Bible Study Notes:

_____
_____
_____
_____
_____
_____
_____
_____
_____
_____
_____
_____
_____
_____

3 John 1:2

"Beloved, I pray that you may prosper in all things and be in health, just as your soul prospers."

Speaker_____

Sermon Title: _____ Date:_____

Romans 8:6

"For to be carnally minded is death, but to be spiritually minded is life and peace."

Sunday School Notes: _____ Date:_____

_____
_____
_____
_____
_____
_____
_____
_____
_____
_____
_____
_____

Bible Study Notes:

_____
_____
_____
_____
_____
_____
_____
_____
_____
_____
_____
_____
_____

Ephesians 4:26

"Be angry, and do not sin": do not let the sun go down on your wrath."

Speaker_____

Sermon Title: _____Date:_____

Matthew 6:14

"For if you forgive men their trespasses, your heavenly Father will also forgive you."

Sunday School Notes: _____ Date:_____

_____
_____
_____
_____
_____
_____
_____
_____
_____
_____

Bible Study Notes:

_____
_____
_____
_____
_____
_____
_____
_____
_____
_____

Proverbs 15:1

"A soft answer turns away wrath, but a harsh word stirs up anger."

Speaker_____

Sermon Title: _____Date:_____

I Peter 5:7

"Casting all your care upon Him, for He cares for you."

Sunday School Notes: _____ Date:_____

_____
_____
_____
_____
_____
_____
_____
_____
_____
_____
_____

Bible Study Notes:

_____
_____
_____
_____
_____
_____
_____
_____
_____
_____
_____

Hebrews 13:8

"Jesus Christ is the same yesterday, today, and forever."

Speaker_____

Sermon Title: _____ Date:_____

Isaiah 53:5

"But He was wounded for our transgressions, He was bruised for our iniquities; The Chastisement for our peace was upon Him, And by His stripes we are healed."

Sunday School Notes: _____ Date:_____

_____
_____
_____
_____
_____
_____
_____
_____
_____
_____
_____
_____

Bible Study Notes:

_____
_____
_____
_____
_____
_____
_____
_____
_____
_____
_____
_____

Psalm 37:25

"I have been young, and now am old; yet I have not seen the righteous forsaken, nor his descendants begging bread."

Speaker_____

Sermon Title: _____ Date:_____

John 3:16

"For God so loved the world that He gave His only begotten Son, that whosoever believes in Him should not perish but have everlasting life."

Sunday School Notes: _____ Date:_____

_____
_____
_____
_____
_____
_____
_____
_____
_____
_____
_____

Bible Study Notes:

_____
_____
_____
_____
_____
_____
_____
_____
_____
_____
_____
_____
_____

James 4:7

"Therefore submit to God. Resist the devil and he will flee from you."

Speaker:_____

Sermon Title: _____Date:_____

Romans 12:21

"Do not be overcome by evil, but overcome evil with good."

Sunday School Notes: _____ Date:_____

_____
_____
_____
_____
_____
_____
_____
_____
_____
_____
_____

Bible Study Notes:

_____
_____
_____
_____
_____
_____
_____
_____
_____
_____
_____
_____
_____

Psalm 34:8

"Oh, taste and see that the Lord is good; blessed is the man who trusts in Him!"

Speaker_____

Sermon Title: _____ Date:_____

Psalm 103:2

"Bless the Lord, O my soul, and forget not all his benefits."

Sunday School Notes: _____ Date:_____

_____
_____
_____
_____
_____
_____
_____
_____
_____
_____
_____

Bible Study Notes:

_____
_____
_____
_____
_____
_____
_____
_____
_____
_____
_____
_____

Psalm 30:5

"Weeping may endure for a night, but joy comes in the morning."

Speaker_____

Sermon Title: _____ Date:_____

_____

Philippians 4:19

"My God shall supply all your needs according to his riches in Glory by Christ Jesus."

Sunday School Notes: _____ Date:_____

_____
_____
_____
_____
_____
_____
_____
_____
_____
_____
_____

Bible Study Notes:

_____
_____
_____
_____
_____
_____
_____
_____
_____
_____
_____
_____
_____

Colossians 3:23

"Whatever you do, do it heartily, as to the Lord."

Speaker_____

Sermon Title: _____Date:_____

2 Timothy 1:7

"God has not given us a spirit of fear, but of power, and of love and a sound mind."

Sunday School Notes: _____ Date:_____

_____
_____
_____
_____
_____
_____
_____
_____
_____
_____
_____

Bible Study Notes:

_____
_____
_____
_____
_____
_____
_____
_____
_____
_____
_____

Isaiah 26:3

"You will keep him in perfect peace, whose mind is stayed on You, because he trusts in You."

Speaker_____

Sermon Title: _____Date:_____

Mark 11:24

"Whatever things you ask when you pray, believe you receive them, and you will have them."

Sunday School Notes: _____ Date:_____

_____
_____
_____
_____
_____
_____
_____
_____
_____
_____
_____

Bible Study Notes:

_____
_____
_____
_____
_____
_____
_____
_____
_____
_____
_____
_____

Romans 12:2

"Do not be conformed to this world but be transformed by the renewing of your mind."

Speaker_____

Sermon Title: _____Date:_____

Ecclesiastes 3:1

"To everything there is a season, a time for every purpose under heaven."

Sunday School Notes: _____ Date:_____

_____
_____
_____
_____
_____
_____
_____
_____
_____
_____
_____

Bible Study Notes:

_____
_____
_____
_____
_____
_____
_____
_____
_____
_____
_____
_____

2 Corinthians 5:21

"For He made Him who knew no sin to be sin for us, that we might become the righteousness of God in Him.

Speaker_____

Sermon Title: _____Date:_____

John 8:32, 36

"And you shall know the truth, and the truth shall make you free. Therefore if the Son makes you free, you shall be free indeed."

Speaker_____

Sermon Title: _____Date:_____

Luke 10:19

"Behold, I give you the authority to trample on serpents and scorpions, and over all the power of the enemy, and nothing shall by any means hurt you."

Sunday School Notes: _____ Date:_____

Bible Study Notes:

2 Corinthians 5:17

"Therefore, if anyone is in Christ, he is a new creation; old things have passed away; behold, all things have become new.

Speaker_____

Sermon Title: _____ Date:_____

Mark 16:17

"And these signs will follow those who believe: In My name they will cast out demons: they will speak with new tongues."

Sunday School Notes: _____ Date:_____

_____
_____
_____
_____
_____
_____
_____
_____
_____
_____
_____

Bible Study Notes:

_____
_____
_____
_____
_____
_____
_____
_____
_____
_____

Revelation 12:11

"And they overcame him by the blood of the Lamb and by the word of their testimony, and they did not love their lives to the death."

Speaker_____

Sermon Title: _____Date:_____

Psalm 37:4

"Delight yourself also in the Lord, And He shall give you the desires of your heart."

Sunday School Notes: _____ Date: _____

_____

_____

_____

_____

_____

_____

_____

_____

_____

_____

_____

Bible Study Notes:

_____

_____

_____

_____

_____

_____

_____

_____

_____

_____

Church Announcements

Church Announcements

Church Announcements

Church Announcements

Church Announcements

Church Announcements

Church Announcements

2013 Calendar

JANUARY
M T W T F S S
    1 2 3 4 5 6
7 8 9 10 11 12 13
14 15 16 17 18 19 20
21 22 23 24 25 26 27
28 29 30 31

FEBRUARY
M T W T F S S
              1 2 3
4 5 6 7 8 9 10
11 12 13 14 15 16 17
18 19 20 21 22 23 24
25 26 27 28

MARCH
M T W T F S S
              1 2 3
4 5 6 7 8 9 10
11 12 13 14 15 16 17
18 19 20 21 22 23 24
25 26 27 28 29 30 31

APRIL
M T W T F S S
1 2 3 4 5 6 7
8 9 10 11 12 13 14
15 16 17 18 19 20 21
22 23 24 25 26 27 28
29 30

MAY
M T W T F S S
    1 2 3 4 5
6 7 8 9 10 11 12
13 14 15 16 17 18 19
20 21 22 23 24 25 26
27 28 29 30 31

JUNE
M T W T F S S
                  1 2
3 4 5 6 7 8 9
10 11 12 13 14 15 16
17 18 19 20 21 22 23
24 25 26 27 28 29 30

JULY
M T W T F S S
1 2 3 4 5 6 7
8 9 10 11 12 13 14
15 16 17 18 19 20 21
22 23 24 25 26 27 28
29 30 31

AUGUST
M T W T F S S
           1 2 3 4
5 6 7 8 9 10 11
12 13 14 15 16 17 18
19 20 21 22 23 24 25
26 27 28 29 30 31

SEPTEMBER
M T W T F S S
                    1
2 3 4 5 6 7 8
9 10 11 12 13 14 15
16 17 18 19 20 21 22
23 24 25 26 27 28 29
30

OCTOBER
M T W T F S S
  1 2 3 4 5 6
7 8 9 10 11 12 13
14 15 16 17 18 19 20
21 22 23 24 25 26 27
28 29 30 31

NOVEMBER
M T W T F S S
              1 2 3
4 5 6 7 8 9 10
11 12 13 14 15 16 17
18 19 20 21 22 23 24
25 26 27 28 29 30

DECEMBER
M T W T F S S
                    1
2 3 4 5 6 7 8
9 10 11 12 13 14 15
16 17 18 19 20 21 22
23 24 25 26 27 28 29
30 31

TO DO LIST

Phone Calls

Errands

Correspondence/e-mail

Church Projects

TO DO LIST

Phone Calls

Errands

Correspondence/e-mail

Church Projects

TO DO LIST

Phone Calls

Errands

Correspondence/e-mail

Church Projects

TO DO LIST

Phone Calls

Errands

Correspondence/e-mail

Church Projects

TO DO LIST

Phone Calls

Errands

Correspondence/e-mail

Church Projects

TO DO LIST

Phone Calls

Errands

Correspondence/e-mail

Church Projects

TO DO LIST

Phone Calls

Errands

Correspondence/e-mail

Church Projects

TO DO LIST

Phone Calls

Errands

Correspondence/e-mail

Church Projects

TO DO LIST

Phone Calls

Errands

Correspondence/e-mail

Church Projects

TO DO LIST

Phone Calls

Errands

Correspondence/e-mail

Church Projects

TO DO LIST

Phone Calls

Errands

Correspondence/e-mail

Church Projects

TO DO LIST

Phone Calls

Errands

Correspondence/e-mail

Church Projects

CONTACT LIST

NAME

ADDRESS

PHONE

E-MAIL

NAME

ADDRESS

PHONE

E-MAIL

NAME

ADDRESS

PHONE

E-MAIL

NAME

ADDRESS

PHONE

E-MAIL

NAME

ADDRESS

PHONE

E-MAIL

NAME

ADDRESS

PHONE

E-MAIL

CONTACT LIST

NAME

ADDRESS

PHONE

E-MAIL

NAME

ADDRESS

PHONE

E-MAIL

NAME

ADDRESS

PHONE

E-MAIL

NAME

ADDRESS

PHONE

E-MAIL

NAME

ADDRESS

PHONE

E-MAIL

NAME

ADDRESS

PHONE

E-MAIL

CONTACT LIST

NAME

ADDRESS

PHONE

E-MAIL

NAME

ADDRESS

PHONE

E-MAIL

NAME

ADDRESS

PHONE

E-MAIL

NAME

ADDRESS

PHONE

E-MAIL

NAME

ADDRESS

PHONE

E-MAIL

NAME

ADDRESS

PHONE

E-MAIL

CONTACT LIST

NAME

ADDRESS

PHONE

E-MAIL

NAME

ADDRESS

PHONE

E-MAIL

NAME

ADDRESS

PHONE

E-MAIL

NAME

ADDRESS

PHONE

E-MAIL

NAME

ADDRESS

PHONE

E-MAIL

NAME

ADDRESS

PHONE

E-MAIL

CONTACT LIST

NAME

ADDRESS

PHONE

E-MAIL

NAME

ADDRESS

PHONE

E-MAIL

NAME

ADDRESS

PHONE

E-MAIL

NAME

ADDRESS

PHONE

E-MAIL

NAME

ADDRESS

PHONE

E-MAIL

NAME

ADDRESS

PHONE

E-MAIL

CONTACT LIST

NAME

ADDRESS

PHONE

E-MAIL

NAME

ADDRESS

PHONE

E-MAIL

NAME

ADDRESS

PHONE

E-MAIL

NAME

ADDRESS

PHONE

E-MAIL

NAME

ADDRESS

PHONE

E-MAIL

NAME

ADDRESS

PHONE

E-MAIL

CONTACT LIST

NAME

ADDRESS

PHONE

E-MAIL

NAME

ADDRESS

PHONE

E-MAIL

NAME

ADDRESS

PHONE

E-MAIL

NAME

ADDRESS

PHONE

E-MAIL

NAME

ADDRESS

PHONE

E-MAIL

NAME

ADDRESS

PHONE

E-MAIL

CONTACT LIST

NAME

ADDRESS

PHONE

E-MAIL

NAME

ADDRESS

PHONE

E-MAIL

NAME

ADDRESS

PHONE

E-MAIL

NAME

ADDRESS

PHONE

E-MAIL

NAME

ADDRESS

PHONE

E-MAIL

NAME

ADDRESS

PHONE

E-MAIL

About the Author

Chaplain Yolanda Walker is a native of Nashville, Tennessee. She is an ordained minister. She holds a Bachelor's Degree from Tennessee State University. In 1998, she was accepted into Morehouse School of Religion at the Interdenominational Theological Center (ITC) of Atlanta, Georgia where she graduated with a Master of Divinity in Psychology of Religion and Pastoral Care. In addition to her degrees, she has completed additional graduate course work at Trevecca Nazarene University in Marriage and Family Therapy. While in Seminary she completed a Unit of Clinical Pastoral Education (CPE) at the Emory and Crawford Long Hospitals and later became an On Call Chaplain for both hospitals. She has had the opportunity of serving in ministry for Baptist, Methodist, and Church of God in Christ Denominations. Chaplain Walker has served as a Pastoral Counselor with the Pastoral Counselor Centers of Tennessee. She has counseled youth, women and men in the area of recovery, abuse, anger management, and substance abuse.

Chaplain Walker serves as Chaplain and Volunteer Coordinator for the Tennessee Prison for Women. She is the Co-Founder and Executive Director for Tri-Fold Outreach, which is a ministry whose mission is to provide Christian Counseling, Curriculum Resources, and Community Outreach Services to inmates, ex-offenders, and the community. Chaplain Walker is a Registered Addiction Specialist Intern with the Breining Institute and has had membership in the following organizations: American Association of Christian Counselors, Tennessee Correctional Association, and Association for Probation and Parole. And, she is an Independent Associate with Legal Shield.

Chaplain Walker has been quoted and/or featured in CBS News, ABC News Online, The Christian Post, Christian Trinity Network (CTN) "The Bridges Show," and the Trinity Broadcasting Network (TBN) Second Chance for Prisoners. She is a gifted speaker, life coach, teacher, counselor, and intercessor. Her passion is to help bring healing and restoration to individual lives that have been wounded through addictions, abuse, relationships and incarceration. God has given her a great assignment to help those who have been forgotten and many cases left for dead. With God's help she will continue to pursue avenues to reach the lost and disenfranchised for the Kingdom Of God through Jesus Christ. She resides in Nashville, Tennessee and is the proud mother of one lovely daughter.

Additional Books

by Chaplain Yolanda Walker

The Adventures of

Wonder Turtle

Let's Go Fishing!

Where is my Mommy?

Children's Book

YOLANDA WALKER

Poetry for The Soul!
Prison Poetry

This book contains poems, quotes from renowned leaders, and resources to help those who are incarcerated.

THANK YOU

Thank you for your purchase. All of our books can be purchased online through Amazon and some through Kindle Publishing. In addition, if you are in the Nashville Area, you may purchase our books at Walker's Café and Grill 109 Ewing Lane, Nashville, Tennessee.

If this book has been a Blessing to you and you would like to sew a seed to help us to continue to do Outreach Ministry, you may send your donation to the following address:
Tri-Fold Outreach
P.O. Box 53
Whites Creek, Tennessee 37189
(800)664-1793

If you are in need of legal services, please visit our website at www.legalshield.com/hub/yfwalker or e-mail us at yfwalker@legalshield.com